THE
bird·ing
DICTIONARY

WRITTEN AND ILLUSTRATED BY
Rosemary Mosco

Workman Publishing · New York

To my sister, Madeline,
and all the humor she brings into my world.

Workman
Workman Publishing
Hachette Book Group, Inc.
1290 Avenue of the Americas
New York, NY 10104
workman.com

Workman is an imprint of Workman Publishing, a division of
Hachette Book Group, Inc. The Workman name and logo are
registered trademarks of Hachette Book Group, Inc.

Cover illustration by Rosemary Mosco
Design and cover by Rae Ann Spitzenberger

The publisher is not responsible for websites (or their content) that
are not owned by the publisher.

Workman books may be purchased in bulk for business,
educational, or promotional use. For information, please contact
your local bookseller or the Hachette Book Group Special Markets
Department at special.markets@hbgusa.com.

Library of Congress Cataloging-in-Publication Data is available.

ISBN 978-1-5235-2535-5

First Edition May 2025

Printed in China on responsibly sourced paper.

10 9 8 7 6 5 4 3 2 1

Foreword

In recent years, the popularity of birding has exploded. With this renewed enthusiasm has come an increase in the number of high-quality books on the subject, from field guides to natural histories to ruminations on the sociocultural impacts of birds.

This book is not one of them.

What you hold in your hands is a dictionary of birding terms. While the terminology is correct, the definitions are often spurious or, worse yet, silly. I sent the author several letters by certified mail expressing my concerns; after many months, I finally received a single envelope in return. It contained three brown feathers and a clump of common yard grass. I suspect the author may be a goose.

As such, I cannot recommend this volume to any birder who, like me, lacks a sense of humor or a penchant for the absurd. For the joyless among us, I suggest you purchase my deeply researched work, *Lifestyles of Left-footed Sparrows of the Iberian Peninsula.* It is available for the reasonable price of $5,890.99 (shipping not included).

Sincerely,

Professor Hallux A. Whitewash
Hemispingus University // Patagonia, AZ

A

adorbler /ə-ˈdȯr-blər/ ***noun:*** Any bird in the **WOOD-WARBLER** family Parulidae. (The term was coined by author Jeff VanderMeer.) Wood-warblers are small, round, and often brightly colored, and their cuteness is powerful enough to overwhelm even the most hardened soul. You can detect the presence of Adorblers by paying attention to the calls of nearby birders; listen for phrases such as "Oh hello, little buddy" and "Well, look at you," as well as a soft, high-pitched *eeeeeee*.

alcid /ˈal-səd/ *noun:* One of a group of bird species in the family Alcidae, which includes auklets, murres, murrelets, guillemots, and puffins. Many alcids look like someone put men's formal wear on a potato.

Alcid
(Dovekie or
Little Auk)

Potato
(formal)

alpha code /ˈal-fə ˌkōd/ *noun:* A four-letter
abbreviation of a bird's common name. Also
known as a bird code or banding code, it's
part of a system of standardized abbreviations
that enable birders, ornithologists, and bird
banders to take speedy notes and otherwise
communicate quickly. For example, the Scale-
crested Pygmy-Tyrant has an ungainly name,
but you can use the alpha code system and
shorten it to SCPT. Some alpha codes are
straightforward, like RUFF for Ruff and OVEN
for Ovenbird. Some are cute, like BABE for
Barred Becard, BUFF for Bufflehead, and
WHIM for Whimbrel. Some are confusing, like
DOVE for Dovekie (which is not a dove) and
CROW for Crested Owl (which is not a crow).
Some are unfortunate, like LEAK for Lesser
'Akialoa, BLOW for Bare-legged Owl, and
GASH for Galapagos Shearwater. The code
for Dickcissel is exactly what you think it
would be.

altricial /al-ˈtri-shəl/ *adjective:* Hatching out naked and helpless. An altricial chick is unable to walk, care for itself, or perceive the world in a meaningful way. Like a human baby, it's a feeble lump that can only yell and defecate, and yet it's still somehow incredibly cute.

American Robin /ə-ˈmer-ə-kən ˈrä-bən/ *noun:* A device that converts worms into 100-decibel songs outside your bedroom at 4 a.m.

Anhinga /an-ˈhiŋ-gə/ *noun:* A winged creature that can swim with neutral buoyancy, stab its prey to death, launch itself into the air from a submerged position, and soar thousands of feet in the sky. The Anhinga may look like a garden hose attached to a chicken, but only fools underestimate it.

anting /ˈan-tiŋ/ *noun:* A fascinating behavior in which a bird lies down among a nest of ants and allows the insects to crawl all over it, or actively picks up ants in its bill and rubs them on its feathers until it is, presumably, all nice and anty. Ornithologists have advanced many explanations for anting, but it's possible that birds just like to mess with us.

I love this for some reason.

B

bait /ˈbāt/ *verb:* To engage in an unethical practice wherein a photographer releases a live mouse or deploys a mouse-shaped cat toy to lure in a hungry **OWL** and take a close-up photograph. Baiting can cause owls to change their behavior in dangerous ways, leading them to approach humans or chase prey across roads. If you find yourself becoming the type of person who carries around live mice in your pocket just to make owls miserable, you might want to consider a different hobby.

band /'band/ **_verb:_** To attach a lightweight ring of metal or plastic around a bird's leg so that the bird can be identified if it is resighted or recaptured. Bird banding helps scientists understand a species' movements and habits over time. Someone who bands birds in the United States is referred to as a bander; in the United Kingdom, bands are called rings and a bander is known as a ringer. **Legal note:** When you put a ring on a bird, you and the bird are not officially married. True bird marriage involves building a nest and laying eggs, tasks rarely attempted by even the most experienced banders.

Baypoll /ˈbā-pōl/ *noun:* A Bay-breasted Warbler or Blackpoll Warbler in nonbreeding plumage. These two warblers look so similar that some birders lump them together and call them Baypolls. Some Baypolls are easier to identify than others. If a bird has bay-colored flanks, for example, it's a Bay-breasted; if it has yellow feet, it's a Blackpoll. Other individuals are subtler and more confusing. When you encounter a really tricky Baypoll, you have two options: 1) Peer at the particularities of its feather and mandible tones until you get existential and contemplate your life choices, or 2) Skip the identification altogether and go directly to contemplating your life choices, preferably in a soft chair with a cold beer.

beak /'bēk/ *noun:* An anatomical feature of birds that consists of bony projections on the top and bottom jaw surrounded by a sheath of keratin; also known as a bill, if you want to be fancy about it. Birds use their beaks for a variety of purposes, including sensing the world around them, probing for worms and other invertebrates deep in the soil, dispatching winged prey, preening, showing off to a mate, and dissipating excess heat. Human teeth are, comparatively, boring. Someday, scientists will figure out how to give us beaks. Until then, we're doomed to get dirt in our gums every time we try to probe for worms.

Bird Mouth **Human Mouth**

Elegant Useful Awkward Boring

behavioral isolation /bi-ˈhā-vyə-rəl ˌī-sə-ˈlā-shən/ *noun:* A situation in which several groups of animals exhibit incompatible behaviors that keep them from interbreeding, enabling them to maintain their distinctive qualities through time. For example, some species of birds use distinctive songs to attract mates. Though their environments reverberate with a symphony of multiple species' chirps, tweets, and warbles (and sometimes hisses, croaks, and screams, just to pander to the metal fans), they rely on their prospective mates' preference for their group's unique tunes in order to pair up and continue the lineage. If you're a birder and you fall in love with an astronomer who only goes out to watch the skies at night, your relationship might be doomed by behavioral isolation—unless you get really into **NFC RECORDINGS** or **OWLS**.

big year /ˌbig ˈyir/ *noun:* A year in which a birder challenges themself to observe as many species as possible. Some birders spend their big year traveling extensively, attempting to observe thousands of species within the allotted time. Besides big years, birders do big days, big weeks, and big sits (where they remain in one location and try to spot as many species as possible). The existence of the big year implies the existence of an even more challenging "small year" in which a birder spends 365 days hiding from birds.

binoculars /bī-ˈnä-kyə-lərs/ *noun:* A handheld optical device that helps a birder identify birds that are very far away. The word *binoculars* can be a mouthful, so birders shorten it in a variety of ways. Acceptable abbreviations include binocs, binos, nocs, and bins. Unacceptable abbreviations include bus, blars, boars, and boculars.

binomial name /bī-ˈnō-mē-əl ˈnām/

noun: The standardized two-part name for a species according to the scientific system of binomial nomenclature consisting of its genus (capitalized and italicized) and its species (lower case and italicized), often with Latin roots. For instance, European colonizers in what is now North America dubbed one particular bird the American Robin because it resembled the European Robin. However, the two species are not closely related, so scientists refer to the American Robin by the binomial name *Turdus migratorius*, which comes from the Latin words for "poops upon" and "my green Toyota Prius."

birb /ˈbərb/ **noun:** Like a **BIRD**, but cuter.

bird /ˈbərd/ *noun:* A type of animal that is, by all scientific and objective measures, the best one. *verb:* The worthy act of beholding a bird and giving it the time and attention it deserves.

bird by ear /bərd bī ˈir/ *verb:* To identify birds by sound. The world of avian auditory communication is rich, complex, and a joy to explore. The Wood Thrush, for instance, makes a spectacularly elaborate three-part song of rapid and sometimes overlapping notes, so that it sounds like a virtuoso flutist. The Tricolored Heron screams *aaaah!*, *scaaaah!*, and *ungh!*, so that it sounds like it stepped on a LEGO.

bird feeder /ˈbərd ˌfē-dər/ *noun:* An object that you fill with seeds and place outside a window so that you can observe the natural world from the comfort of your home. You'll see hordes of gray squirrels swarm your bird feeder by day and families of flying squirrels empty it out by night. Raccoons will sit on top of it and eat seeds by the fistful, while rats will scarf down whatever falls to the ground. When black bears wake up hungry from hibernation, they'll obliterate your feeder before moving on to your garbage cans. If you're very lucky, you may even attract a bird.

bird festival /ˈbərd ˈfe-stə-vəl/ *noun:* A gathering much like a rock festival, but for birding. Instead of concerts, there are field walks, talks, and photography workshops. Instead of rock stars, there are mild-mannered birding celebrities who'll calmly teach you about sandpiper molts. Instead of poorly behaved rich kids trashing everything, there are gulls.

birder /ˈbər-dər/ *noun:* A person who engages in the hobby of spotting, listening to, and/or otherwise perceiving birds. If you love observing birds, you're a birder. If you're new to the hobby, you're a birder. If you love birds but have never heard any of the slang or scientific jargon in this book before, you're a birder. If you're the type of person who judges other birders for not knowing enough about birds, you're still a birder, but you're also an ass. If you're a Peregrine Falcon and love observing birds, you're just hungry.

blind /ˈblīnd/ *noun:* A small, well-camouflaged shelter in which birders conceal themselves so that they can take close-up photos of birds in the surrounding area without disturbing them; also known as a hide. A blind can be a wooden shack, a tent with a camo print, or even a floating structure with a suspended seat, as long as it's sweaty and uncomfortable. Contrary to popular belief, birds are fully aware that there's a human inside a blind. They just come close because they feel bad for us.

bop around /'bäp ə-'raůnd/ *verb:* To move rapidly from place to place within a particular area. This phrase is often used to describe the movements of small birds, such as warblers, that are hunting for bugs in foliage and never pause long enough to offer **GOOD LOOKS**. Birders will say, with a mix of enthusiasm and weariness, "There sure are a lot of them bopping around in there."

Warbler Motion Within a Bush

borb /ˈbȯrb/ *noun:* A **BIRB** that has fluffed up its feathers such that every surface point is equidistant from a common center point, i.e., a sphere. The volume of a borb is calculated with this formula: $V = (4/3) \pi r^3$, or you can just wait for it to sing and hear how loud it is.

butterbutt /ˈbə-tər-ˌbət/ *noun:* A nickname for the Yellow-rumped Warbler, a small songbird with a butter-yellow rump. When you first hear the word, you'll probably laugh. Over time, however, you'll find yourself regularly declaring "Oh, look, a butterbutt" with absolute seriousness in the company of other humans, thanks to the magic of birding. The Yellow-rumped Warbler also has yellow spots below its wings, but nobody calls it butterpits, and that's a shame.

butterflier /ˈbə-tər-ˌflīr/ *noun:* A person
who enjoys observing butterflies. Birders and
butterfliers can be difficult to distinguish in the
field. Here are their similarities and differences:

Birder	Butterflier
Keeps a list of species seen	Keeps a list of species seen
Is attracted to bright colors and movement	Is attracted to bright colors and movement
Typically points binoculars at trees	Typically points binoculars at the ground
Takes photographs with a telephoto lens	Takes photographs with a macro lens
Doesn't crawl on the ground for photographs unless it's shorebird season	Crawls on the ground for photographs, because butterflies are less likely to startle if you keep below their horizon line
Chugs coffee and hits the road pre-dawn, like a commuter trying to beat traffic	Sleeps in, then sashays into the field midmorning when it's nice and warm, like an aristocrat attending a garden party
Agonizes over empid identification	Agonizes over skipper identification
Sore neck	Sore back

buzzard /ˈbə-zərd/ *noun:* A large bird whose identity varies by location. In the UK, a buzzard is any raptor of the genus *Buteo*. In the US, species in the genus *Buteo* are called hawks; the word *buzzard* is reserved for vultures. This is just one of many cross-Atlantic linguistic differences, and care should be taken to avoid misunderstandings. For instance, in the UK, the word "crisp" is akin to the US word "chip." In the UK, the phrase "That's very interesting" is a kind way to say "That's boring—please stop talking to me," whereas a person from the US would consider this an enthusiastic invitation to keep sharing obscure bird facts until the UK person politely expires.

BVD /ˌbē-(ˌ)vē-ˈdē/ *noun:* Shorthand for Better View Desired, included as part of a birder's report to say that their view of a rare bird was limited to perhaps one toenail, or a few atoms of a feather, or an echo of a chirp that lingered in their ear like the whisper of a long-lost friend.

C

camera /ˈkam-rə/ *noun:* A device that
lets you capture a still image of a bird,
provided that the bird is not too far away,
it stays motionless for long enough, it's facing
toward or perpendicular to you, the lighting
is right, there aren't any twigs between
you and the bird, you've dialed in the right
settings, you've remembered to bring a
memory card with space, your camera battery
is fully charged, you've got the right lens,
the weather is not hazy or foggy, and you
have correctly performed the relevant
arcane rituals.

Canadian Goose /kə-ˈnā-dē-ən ˈgüs/

noun: A commonly used but incorrect name
for the Canada Goose (*Branta canadensis*). If
you hear a fellow birder say "Canadian Goose"
and you're tempted to correct them, consider
the following: Will the person in question enjoy
learning a new fact, or will they feel belittled
and perhaps lose interest in birding? Will you
be doing more harm than good? Should we all
take the time to lose ourselves in the pure joy
of watching wildlife, regardless of whether
we're using the appropriate terminology? Is
the person just trying to distract you while
that Canada Goose creeps closer and closer?
Did the goose slip them a few bucks when you
weren't looking? Are you now being bitten,
hard and repeatedly, by a goose?

car blind /ˈkär blīnd/ *noun:* Any vehicle

from which you view birds. Most birds don't view cars as a threat—perhaps they see vehicles as some sort of large grazing animal— so you can creep up to birds by driving slowly, then roll down the window and take pictures. Just don't open the door and step out. Birds will instantly flee from the horrifying sight of a huge grazing animal giving birth to a human.

catastrophic molt /ka-tə-ˈsträ-fik ˈmōlt/

noun: When a bird molts a large number of its feathers all at once. The word *catastrophic* may seem overly dramatic, but one day you'll find yourself face to face with a cardinal that has lost all of its head feathers and looks like a demon plotting to sell you to Satan for a fistful of suet—then you'll understand.

CBC /ˌsē-bē-ˈsē/ *noun:* Short for Christmas Bird Count, an annual winter survey administered by the National Audubon Society that aims to track changes in bird populations over time. Ornithologist Frank M. Chapman created the CBC in 1900 as an alternative to the Christmas tradition of Side Hunts— shooting every songbird or other small animal you could find, dumping the bodies in a huge pile, and comparing piles to figure out who had the biggest one. Merry Christmas! Nowadays, birders go out during the holidays and count as many live birds as they can in a designated area during a single day. If they've been nice birders, Santa will bring them **GOOD LOOKS** at rare species. If they've been naughty, he'll bring them freezing rain and a few damp starlings.

chase /ˈchās/ *verb:* To travel—sometimes for a great distance—to a place where a rare bird has been spotted and then sneak around trying to catch a glimpse of it. Note: You should never actually *chase* a bird. Experienced birders know that birds often have two wings and can fly up into the sky, a place that is difficult for most humans to access.

chat /ˈchat/ *noun:* 1. One of many songbirds belonging to various unrelated groups. Examples include the Yellow-breasted Chat of North America, the Rose-breasted Chat of north-central South America, and the Familiar Chat of sub-Saharan Africa. 2. A group text that people use to let each other know about a rare bird sighting, or, alternately, to complain that the previous person's bird sighting is not unusual enough to merit a text.

clap /ˈklap/ **verb:** To rapidly bring the palms of your hands together to produce a loud, sharp sound for the purpose of trying to get a **RAIL** to call back at you in a swamp. Should you find yourself outside of a swamp, you can also clap to tell another human that they're doing a good job. If a rail shows up anyway, that's a nice bonus.

Step 1

Step 2

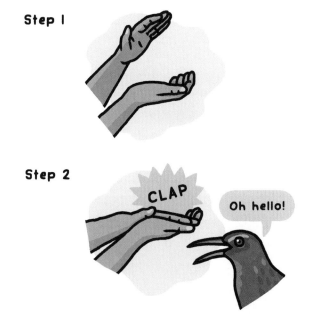

CLAP

Oh hello!

cloaca /klō-ˈā-kə/ *noun:* An all-purpose anatomical chamber that ends in an opening called a vent through which a bird passes waste (both feces and urine-like substances), eggs, and other reproductive material. It might seem strange that birds release everything through one hole, but we humans are, arguably, equally weird for carefully separating our excretions before shooting them out in various directions.

confiding /kən-ˈfī-diŋ/ *adjective:* Unafraid of humans; also described as friendly or obliging. A confiding bird is one that hangs out close to birders, giving them great looks and photo ops. It will not, however, confide any actual secrets. But that's fine, since bird secrets are things like "where to find the juiciest caterpillars" and "how to puke into your kids' mouths."

confusing fall warbler

/kən-'fyü-ziŋ 'fòl 'wòr-blər/ *noun:* **1.** One of a number of **WOOD-WARBLER** species that are difficult to identify during the fall migration; *see* **BAYPOLL**. In autumn, many warblers have shed their brighter, more easily recognizable breeding plumage and are sporting a subtler mix of olives, yellows, and browns, and the recently hatched young can be drab, making both parents and children challenging for birders to identify definitively. **2.** A warbler that refuses to let you enter its forest until you answer a series of perplexing riddles.

conservation biology /ˌkän(t)-sər-

'vā-shən bī-'ä-lə-jē/ *noun:* A deeply complex and nuanced applied scientific field that, in essence, preserves in perpetuity your opportunity to get yarfed on by a California Condor.

contact call /ˈkän-ˌtakt ˈkȯl/ *noun:* A type
of sound that birds make to keep in touch with
each other; frequently used by members of
the same family group while they're exploring
or feeding. These conversations can be
translated as:

"You good?"

"Yeah. You still alive?"

"Yup. Any tasty bugs over there?"

"Yeah. Any tasty bugs over there?"

"Yeah. You still a bird?"

*"Let me check: I have two wings and a
beak, so yes. You still a bird?"*

*"I think so. Let me check. Two wings and a
beak over here. You got feathers as well?"*

"Yup. Feathers. You?"

"Also feathers."

"Great. You good?"

"Yeah. You good?"

"Yeah. Any bugs over there?"

And so on and so forth.

continuing /kən-'tin-yü-iŋ/ *adjective:*

Present at a given location after also being seen on previous days; used to describe a rare bird that hasn't moved on from the place it was first sighted, probably because it's too embarrassed to admit that it's lost.

contour /'kän-ˌtu̇r/ *adjective:* Describing the outer feathers that cover a bird. These feathers define its streamlined shape and enhance its aerodynamism. *verb:* To apply makeup such that it highlights and enshadows particular areas of the face. This technique changes the face's apparent shape but has no impact on its aerodynamism.

convergent evolution /kən-ˈvər-jənt ˌe-və-ˈlü-shən/ *noun:* A form of plagiarism in which two unrelated species develop similar characteristics. For instance, swallows and swifts independently evolved small bodies, long pointed wings, and short legs. Either one of them could file an intellectual property lawsuit against the other and be awarded millions of bugs in damages.

Swallow   Swift

Plagiarism?!

coop /ˈküp/ *noun:* 1. A nickname for the Cooper's Hawk, a medium-sized hawk in the genus *Accipiter* whose diet is often dominated by birds. 2. A small structure full of chickens that a Cooper's Hawk wants to be inside of.

courtship /ˈkȯrt-ˌship/ *noun:* Behaviors aimed at attracting a mate, including singing, dancing, running around, gathering and presenting food, trying to look big, standing somewhere high up and yelling, and generally making oneself look ridiculous. Much like humans, birds also engage in these behaviors.

covert /ˈkə-vərt/ *noun:* A type of body feather that covers the base of a tail or wing feather, helping to create a smooth, aerodynamic surface on a bird's body. When a bird preens in secret, it's a covert operation.

crop /ˈkräp/ *noun:* An enlarged part of a bird's esophagus that temporarily stores food so that it can be carried away for later consumption in a safe place. A crop is somewhat like a purse, except that instead of half-finished lip balms and old receipts, it's full of seeds, chunks of meat, and sometimes an entire slice of pizza. Or perhaps your purse is also full of those things. No judgment; enjoy the pizza.

crown /ˈkraůn/ *noun:* A patch of colorful
feathers on top of a bird's head that indicates
it is the rightful ruler of the realm. Birds with
crowns signifying royal status include the
Golden-crowned Kinglet, Yellow-crowned
Night Heron, Gray-crowned Rosy Finch, and
more. When you encounter such a bird, you
must curtsy or perform a short bow at the
neck, lest ye be banished from its domain.

crush /ˈkrəsh/ *verb:* To take a fantastic
picture of a desired bird. No actual birds are
injured when a photographer crushes one.
noun: An infatuation with someone, which
will only grow stronger if they take a fantastic
picture of a desired bird.

D

digiscope /ˈdi-jə-ˌskōp/ *verb:* To attach
your camera or phone to your scope or
binoculars so that you can take a picture
of a distant bird. Digiscoping may be finicky
and difficult to master, but when your
alternatives are 1) disturbing the whole flock,
2) trespassing, 3) attempting to approach
the birds and sinking into a swamp, or, most
terribly, 4) not having anyone believe that you
saw a rare bird without the picture to prove it,
your choice is clear.

American
Dipper

American
Dip

American
Dipping

dip /ˈdip/ *verb:* 1. To miss out on a bird sighting, even though you tried so hard to see the bird. Every birder dips at some point. You may hop in the car, drive for hours, and show up just minutes after a bird leaves the area. Or you may learn while en route that a "rare" bird was a misidentified common species.
2. What an American Dipper does. If you miss seeing an American Dipper, that's a double dip.

distraction display /di-ˈstrak-shən di-ˈsplā/ *noun:*

What happens when a predator approaches a nest and a parent bird intentionally lures it away by spreading its tail, dragging a wing, making loud calls, or flying upward suddenly. To understand the concept of a distraction display, try the following activity:

Step 1: Look around and tally up the number of bird chicks you can see.

Step 2: Hand this book to a friend and ask them to read the following sentence aloud: "HEY, PREDATOR, LOOK OVER HERE!"

Step 3: Determine if this display was successful by counting the number of chicks again. If you ate any of them, it failed.

duck /ˈdək/ *noun:* Any bird that paddles around on the water and isn't a goose, loon, swan, grebe, cormorant, Anhinga, coot, gallinule, gull, auklet, murre, murrelet, guillemot, razorbill, puffin, pelican, petrel, storm-petrel, shearwater, albatross, gannet, booby, tropicbird, or eagle that tried to grab a really heavy fish.

dump laying /ˈdəmp ˌlā-iŋ/ *noun:* A

behavior in which a bird lays its eggs in another bird's nest, then departs to avoid any childcare duties; also known as egg dumping. Many species engage in egg dumping, including Wood Ducks, Tree Swallows, and American Avocets. Sometimes multiple birds dump their eggs in a single bird's nest. The owner of the nest doesn't push out the dumped eggs; instead, the mother thinks to itself, *Gosh, I guess those eggs are just reproducing on their own now!* and likely has a wee existential crisis that ends in a rude awakening when all the eggs hatch and suddenly there are forty mouths to feed.

dust bathe /ˈdəst ˌbāt͟h/ **verb:** To roll around in dust, sand, or dirt. Many birds dust bathe, and scientists aren't sure why they do it, but it seems to help them stay clean. It may sop up excess feather oil or kill parasites. Don't try it yourself. When a human dust bathes, she just gets dirt all over her clothes and people say things like "Ma'am, please stop; this is a Starbucks parking lot."

dynamic soaring /dī-ˈna-mik ˈsȯr-iŋ/ **noun:** A complex method of flying whereby albatrosses and other seabirds zigzag above the surface of the ocean, capturing energy from the gradient of wind velocity and using it to fly long distances without experiencing the indignity of having to flap their long goofy wings.

E

eBird /ˈē-ˌbərd/ *noun:* A project of the Cornell Lab of Ornithology in which bird observations submitted by birders and organizations worldwide are collected, reviewed, and presented. Birders use eBird to keep track of their sightings and share them with others. They also browse the database to learn about the birds they may see in a particular area, or to study past trends. It's important to note that eBird is not affiliated with eBay; you cannot use it to buy a PlayStation or bid on rare birds.

eclipse /i-ˈklips/ *noun:* 1. A type of plumage worn by certain male birds—particularly ducks, but also fairy wrens and others—after the mating season. Males shed their colorful feathers and develop duller, less conspicuous patterns that resemble female plumage and help them hide from predators. Birds in eclipse plumage can be harder to identify. 2. A portentous event in which astronomical bodies line up such that they obscure each other. When the moon is positioned between the sun and the earth, it's a solar eclipse. When the earth is positioned between the sun and a large diving bird, it's a loonar eclipse.

egg /ˈeg/ *noun:* A sort of small rock that often has a bird in it.

empid /'empėd/ **noun:** A nickname for any flycatcher belonging to the genus *Empidonax*. Empids are notoriously difficult to tell apart. They're small, gray-olive birds with lighter throats, wing bars, and eye rings, though they differ subtly within these parameters. Helpfully, ornithologists have given these birds distinctive names:

> **White-throated Flycatcher:** Has a whitish throat, like many members of the genus *Empidonax*.

> **Gray Flycatcher:** Has gray on it, like many members of the genus *Empidonax*.

> **Least Flycatcher:** Small, like many members of the genus *Empidonax*. It's a little smaller than usual, though.

Empids are best told apart when they sing, which they prefer not to do.

Alder Flycatcher, probably

F

fallout /ˈfȯl-ˌau̇t/ *noun:* 1. A thing that birders celebrate and nuclear scientists fear. Fallout occurs when migrating birds encounter inclement weather and "fall out" of the sky to rest in large numbers, thrilling birders. 2. When radioactive particles "fall out" of the sky following a nuclear blast, causing widespread destruction and creating conditions unfavorable for birding. Like **STAKEOUT**, **LIFER**, and **SPECULUM**, fallout is one of those words that you'd rather hear out of a birder's mouth than anybody else's.

feather /ˈfe-_th_ər/ **noun:** A type of foliage that grows on a bird. It consists of a rigid central part, or stem, surrounded by a softer part, or leaf. A feather has many purposes; it can be used to fly, to camouflage, to provide warmth, to communicate, or to pen a tragic novel by candlelight while staring across the misty moors, brooding.

feather tract /ˈfe-thər ˌtrakt/ *noun:*

1. A region of a bird's skin from which feathers grow. **2.** A religious brochure written with the goal of convincing more people to perform The Ritual and pledge their souls to the Warbler King for all eternity.

WARNING: *If you think that baby birds are cute, and you'd like to continue to think so, please skip the following definition and start reading again after the triple asterisk.*

fecal sac /ˈfē-kəl ˈsak/ *noun:* A type of waste produced by young birds composed of a blob of fecal matter in a thick, sac-like mucus membrane. Early in a chick's life, its parents will harvest the fecal sacs while they're being extruded and then consume them, since they contain enough partially digested food to be nutritionally valuable. As a chick ages, the parents will begin to carry the sacs away from the nest, depositing them in bodies of water such as ponds or backyard pools.

***

End of warning. Have a lovely day! And just a thought—maybe you should clean your pool.

Female Bird Day /ˌfē-māl ˈbərd ˈdā/

noun: A celebration of female birds that takes place annually at the end of May. This event was started by a group of birders, writers, conservationists, and scientists who call themselves the Galbatrosses. Female Bird Day aims to gather information about, and focus attention on, female birds. Scientists are only just beginning to study female birdsong, and English-language common names for birds often skew male; the female Red-winged Blackbird, for instance, is mostly brown. These biases have consequences for conservation efforts. In some species, males and females occupy different habitats at certain times of the year, but male-focused conservation plans leave the females open to threats. Some readers may find this situation surprising. Others are rolling their eyes and muttering "of course" with a soul-deep weariness.

ferruginous /fə-ˈrü-jə-nəs/ *adjective:*

Rusty in color. This word can be found in many bird names, such as the Ferruginous Duck, Ferruginous Hawk, Ferruginous Antbird, and Ferruginous Pygmy-Owl. It stems from the Latin word *ferrum*, meaning "iron." When exposed to water and oxygen, a ferruginous bird oxidizes, turning to rust; the Ferruginous Pygmy-Owl, for instance, is just a Northern Pygmy-Owl that has spent too long in the rain.

field guide /ˈfēld ˈgīd/ *noun:* A type of book that birders compulsively collect, like dragons hoarding a pile of precious treasure. When a new guide comes out, they'll buy it immediately, no matter the subject—whether it's broad in scope like *Birds of Australia* or obscure like *Shrike-Tits of Southern Australia Who Are Ambivalent about Cilantro*. They'll take it home and add it to their pile, upon which they will sit, twitching their tails and hissing in satisfaction.

field mark /ˈfēld ˈmärk/ *noun:* A distinguishing physical characteristic used to help identify a bird. Field guides often indicate field marks with small arrows or bits of text, but be aware that these words and arrows are rarely found on birds in the wild.

flush /ˈfləsh/ *verb:* To spook a bird out into the open. Some birders intentionally flush rare birds so that they can get **GOOD LOOKS**; most people consider this behavior unethical since it wastes a bird's precious energy. Now and then, however, you may accidentally flush a bird while you're just walking along out in nature. When that happens, the best course of action is to feel embarrassed, exclaim, "Aah, I'm sorry, I'm so sorry," and then remember that birds can't understand human language and feel even more embarrassed.

54

FOY /ˌef-ō-ˈwī/ *noun:* An acronym for First of Year, an expression used to indicate the first time a birder sees a species during a calendar year. Other related acronyms include:

FOS: First of Season

LOY: Last of Year

LOS: Last of Season

FOOY: First Oriole of Year

FOOOY: First Orchard Oriole of Year

FOOOOY: First Obvious Orchard Oriole of Year

FOMO: Fear of Missing Orioles

FPS: Finches Per Season

FUBAR: First Unicolored Blackbird at Refuge

FWIW: First Waxwing in Winter

FOIA: Freedom of Information Anhinga

freezer /ˈfrē-zər/ *noun:* The cold part of a refrigerator where an ornithologist stores ice cubes, frozen meals, and the dead birds that they have found and plan to donate to a local museum or university once they've got a spare afternoon. If you're hanging out at an ornithologist's house and they offer you a beverage, decline the ice.

fulvous /ˈfŭl-vəs/ *adjective:* Tawny or orangey-brown. This word appears in many bird names, such as the Fulvous Whistling-Duck, the Fulvous Owl, the Fulvous-dotted Treerunner, the Fulvous Parrotbill, the Fulvous-breasted Flatbill, the Fulvous-crowned Scrub-Tyrant, the Fulvous Hawk-Eagle, and the Fulvous-chinned Nunlet.*

---

* One of these bird names is fake. Can you guess which one?

G

gashawk /'gas-ˌhȯk/ *noun:* Slang term for aircraft. Gashawks are easily distinguished from goshawks because they rarely show barring on their underparts (or streaking, in juveniles) and because they don't flap their wings very much (unless something has gone terribly wrong).

gestalt /gə-'stält/ *noun:* A fancy German word referring to the general shape and impression of a bird. Use it to opine about a bird's identification so you can sound erudite without having to recall any **FIELD MARKS**.

gleaning /ˈglēn-iŋ/ *noun:* A behavior in which a bird picks invertebrates from surfaces such as leaves, bark, and rock faces. Warblers, nuthatches, kinglets, and many other species glean. Some bird species are even named in part for their habit of picking insects from leaves. The White-collared Foliage-gleaner, for instance, is a bird that gleans insects from foliage on its lunch break before tightening its tie and stepping back into the office to run a few meetings and perhaps commit some light securities fraud.

glossy /ˈglä-sē/ *adjective:* Describing any bird, such as a Glossy Ibis, Glossy Starling, or Glossy-mantled Manucode, to which a shiny top coat has been applied.

good bird /ˌgu̇d ˈbərd/ *noun:* A bird that birders are excited to see, usually because it's rare for the area. The word *good* does not indicate that the bird is morally superior. For instance, a Bald Eagle is labeled a good bird if it has wandered into an area where its species is uncommonly found, even if it's there to steal food from a hungry Osprey, build a structurally unsound nest, or eat a cute duck.

good looks /ˌgu̇d ˈlu̇ks/ *noun:* Excellent opportunities to view a particular bird. What constitutes a good look can vary. A birder will say "I got good looks!" when a common species lands just a few feet away and poses in full sunlight or when a rare species hops between two branches and displays a field mark for the amount of time it takes a **HUMMINGBIRD** to blink.

goose /ˈgüs/ *noun:* A DUCK with a larger bite radius.

GREG /'greg/ *noun:* A four-letter abbreviation for Great Egret drawn from the official list of **ALPHA CODES**. Birders may casually call this species Greg. When you're angry at a Great Egret, use the more formal Gregory.

grip /'grip/ *verb:* To observe a bird that someone else wanted to see and then brag about it; from British birding slang. *noun:* One of several hand positions that trained bird banders use to hold a bird so that neither the bander nor the bird is injured. Commonly used grips include, but are not limited to:

- Pencil grip, used for hummingbirds
- Bander's grip, used for a variety of species
- Photographer's grip, used to secure a bird for the purpose of photographic documentation
- Ice-cream cone grip, used for **RAPTORS**, kingfishers, and other larger birds

Note: Never confuse a raptor for an ice-cream cone and go in for a lick.

gull /'gəl/ *noun:* A bird in the suborder Lari that nests in large colonies, has webbed feet, and makes squawking calls. Many gulls are spectacularly patterned. The Ivory Gull gleams as white as Arctic snow; Sabine's Gull has a black bill with a sunshine-yellow tip; the Swallow-tailed Gull sports shocking red eye rings; the Lava Gull looks like it's dusted with volcanic ash. Gulls are intelligent and behaviorally flexible. Their diet includes fish stolen from other birds, sandwiches stolen from tourists, and chunks of skin stolen from whales. Their piercing calls have inspired human imitators. In Belgium, the European Championship Gullscreeching contest invites individuals or groups (dubbed "colonies") to compete for best screech. All told, gulls are fierce, beautiful, shocking, and fun to watch. If you're not careful, they'll steal your heart. Then they'll carry it to some poop-covered rock and eat it.

H

habitat /ˈha-bə-ˌtat/ *noun:* An area that contains all the resources necessary for a particular species' survival. Some examples of birds and their habitats include:

Ruffed Grouse	Aspen forests and early successional mixed forests with small clearings
Acorn Woodpecker	Oak forests, particularly those with a high diversity of oak species
Great-tailed Grackle	A parking lot at dusk outside a Texas supermarket
Herring Gull	Wherever a small child has left an open bag of Fritos on a beach towel
Spruce Grouse	The other side of the bog from wherever you're currently birding

Hawk Watch /ˈhȯk ˈwäch/ *noun:* A

gathering of people, often on a mountaintop, who watch hawks migrate overhead and record their species and numbers. A Hawk Watch is a safe and fun activity, but if officials upgrade it to a Hawk Warning, seek shelter immediately and wear goggles to protect your eyes from the slashing talons.

hawking /ˈhȯk-iŋ/ *noun:* A behavior in

which a bird flies out from a perch, grabs an insect to eat, and returns to its perch. Birds that hunt by hawking include flycatchers, catbirds, warblers, bee-eaters, waxwings, fantails, and more. Birds that do not hunt by hawking include hawks.

Nighthawk (Not a Hawk) Hawking

heron /'her-ən/ *noun:* A spring-loaded blade on stilts that stabs fish and frogs to death and looks majestic while doing it.

herper /'hər-pər/ *noun:* Like a **BIRDER**, but for reptiles and amphibians. The study of herps is technically called herpetology, and people who search for herps on a casual basis are known as herpers. If you encounter a person who is lifting up rocks or logs and peering under them, they're either a herper or a *really* ineffective birder. Herpers are quick to point out that birds are technically herps, since all birds descended from reptiles. Birders, however, are quick to point out that they don't regularly get peed on by toads.

hotspot /ˈhät-ˌspät/ *noun:* A public birding location listed on the Cornell Lab of Ornithology's eBird database. If you go to a birding hotspot expecting Wi-Fi, you'll be disappointed, but you might get great WIFL (Willow Flycatcher).

Hudwit /ˈhəd-ˌwit/ *noun:* Short for Hudsonian Godwit, a large shorebird with long legs and a slightly upturned bill that nests in the Arctic and winters in the southern part of South America. Use the word *Hudwit* when you're excited to see a Hudsonian Godwit but you're also a busy person with important places to be.

hummingbird /ˈhə-miŋ-ˌbərd/ *noun:*

A bee that has successfully tricked everyone into thinking it's a bird.

hybrid /ˈhī-brəd/ *noun:* A bird that is a mix

of two species. Compared to other groups of animals, birds hybridize with surprising regularity. Some scientists think this high frequency of hybridization helps birds evolve rapidly and take advantage of environmental changes. Most scientists, however, are too cowardly to admit that hybridization is a conspiracy by Big Bird to keep rolling out new models so that birders don't lose interest in the brand.

I

IBA /ˌī-(ˌ)bē-ˈā/ *noun:* Short for Important Bird Area, a region that is of critical importance to birds. Spearheaded by BirdLife International and supported by partners around the world, the IBA program works to identify, monitor, and protect areas that are essential to avian survival. IBA is also short for Iron Butt Association, a group of people who promote extreme long-distance motorcycle riding, in case you're a motorcyclist and you picked up the wrong book. Hopefully your butt is okay.

ID /ˈī-ˈdē/ *noun:* 1. Short for identification; the determination of a bird's species. 2. A document that you show to a bouncer before entering any bird sanctuary that has a liquor license.

In that tree over there, the one with the big fork; no, the other one with the fork; that tree with the really pale bark; about halfway up, or maybe two-thirds of the way up; on the right side, at the end of the second-longest branch; see, it just flew; oh you didn't see it? well, now it's in the pine tree; no, the other pine tree, the big one with the split top, near that dead branch; oh come on, how come you still can't see it? it's right there; oh no, it flew away /ˈyīks/ *noun:*

Where the bird was.

in the field /ˌin thə ˈfēld/ *noun:* Out in nature; referring to the conditions experienced when one is visiting a forest, shrubland, bog, fen, swamp, brush, prairie, desert, tundra, jungle, mountain, sea, stream, lake, ocean, or, sometimes, field.

International Guillemot Appreciation Day

/in-tər-ˈna-sh(ə-)nəl ˈgi-lə-ˌmät ə-ˌprē-shē-ˈā-shən ˈdā/ ***noun:*** A holiday that would be eagerly anticipated by children all over the world if they knew what the heck a guillemot was. Also known as IGAD and traditionally observed on June 27, this event is the brainchild of seabird biologists on Matinicus Rock, a remote, treeless island 23 miles off the coast of Maine, where the windswept isolation presumably causes one's mind to wander. The event celebrates the three seabird species in the genus *Cepphus*: the Pigeon Guillemot, Black Guillemot, and Spectacled Guillemot. Can you imagine a life without guillemots? It would be an empty life, probably, so mark your calendars!

introduced /ˌin-trə-ˈdüst/ *adjective:*

1. Refers to a species that people have transported, either intentionally or accidentally, into a new area. Some of these introduced species have little impact on their new environment; others damage the ecosystem by eating local species, spreading diseases, or altering the habitat. For instance, feral cats introduced into formerly predator-free islands have driven many bird species to extinction.

2. Having previously become acquainted with someone, perhaps a fellow birder at some good birding spot, but now you've run into them again and you can't remember their name to save your life, and you *know* you have no excuse because you do recall that you were both looking for the one Stilt Sandpiper amongst a flock of yellowlegs, and if you can remember *that*, why can't you remember a simple human name, *arrrrrrgh.*

irruption /i-ˈrəp-shən/ *noun:* A phenomenon in which large numbers of birds spread out from their typical **RANGES**. Irruptions have complex causes that are connected to food abundance. For instance, northern conifer trees produce cones in cycles, resulting in seasons of feast or famine for the birds that eat them. When food is sparse, finches such as Evening Grosbeaks and Common Redpolls venture farther south in search of sustenance, delighting birders who are usually unable to view these species. An *irruption* is not to be confused with an *eruption*, which occurs when enough birds build up below the earth's crust that it ruptures, spewing huge amounts of birds into the air at high temperatures and speeds.

J

jealousy /ˈje-lə-sē/ *noun:* An unpleasant feeling that arises from all sorts of situations—some economic and deeply interpersonal—but chiefly when your friend tells you, "The bird was JUST here."

jizz /ˈjiz/ *noun:* Also spelled giss, an unfortunate term that refers to the complex mix of characteristics used to identify a species; similar to GESTALT. Many birders prefer instead to use terms like "impression" or "vibes," and who can blame them?

K

kettle /ˈke-tᵊl/ *noun:* A group of birds—often migrating **RAPTORS** such as Broad-winged Hawks, Sharp-shinned Hawks, Swainson's Hawks, or Bald Eagles—that whirl within a rising column of hot air like bubbles in a kettle of boiling water. If you love watching a pot boil but wish you could spend a whole morning staring at each individual bubble from a long distance away and trying to distinguish it from all the other bubbles, then you may enjoy a **HAWK WATCH**.

kleptoparasitism /ˌklep-tə-ˈper-ə-sə-ˌti-zəm/ **noun:** A behavior in which a bird steals food that another animal has gathered. (Frigatebirds steal food from boobies, tropicbirds, and other species. Bald Eagles steal from Ospreys. Coots steal from ducks.) Kleptoparasitism comes from the Greek terms *klepto*, meaning "steal," and *parasitos*, meaning "someone who eats at another's table," so try to find comfort in this fancy etymology the next time a gull steals your fries.

L

LBJ /ˌel-(ˌ)bē-ˈjā/ *noun:* 1. The short form of little brown job, which is a dismissive term referring to one of many small birds that are frustratingly difficult to identify, such as wrens and sparrows. 2. The short form of Lyndon Baines Johnson, the 36th president of the United States, who is easily distinguished from other LBJs by his lack of a beak.

lens /ˈlenz/ *noun:* The part of a camera that collects and focuses light. Birding photographers use various types of lenses, from telephotos to macros to wide angles to primes, depending on the scene they'd like to capture. Try this trick: If you're going on a nature outing, accidentally leave one of your lenses at home, and you'll be guaranteed to see something interesting that would have been best captured with that lens.

lens cloth /ˈlenz ˌklȯth/ *noun:* A decorative piece of fabric that serves as a fun collectible item. It's recommended to purchase several of them so they can sit at the bottom of your bag or in the back of your drawer, always too far away when you actually need to clean a lens.

license plate /ˈlī-sᵊn(t)s ˈplāt/ *noun:* A

metal identification plate. As a driver, you are legally required to place a license plate on your car. As a birder, you are legally required to come up with a bird-related vanity plate for your car. Here are a few options:

Beginner License Plates	Advanced License Plates
BIRDIN	L1MPK1N
I BIRD	OOLOGY
B1RDER	EMP1DZ
SONGBRD	B1TTRN
CHICKADEE	MUDB4T
GLDFNCH	G1LEMOT
WARBLR	TUBENOZ
CRD1N4L	CLO4C4

Personalizing your license plate is a great way to help other birders recognize you even when you're hiding inside your **CAR BLIND**.

lick /'lik/ ***noun:*** A place where birds congregate to consume substances, such as clay, that are rich in essential minerals and are otherwise lacking in the birds' diets of seeds and fruit. In the Amazon, for instance, birders gleefully congregate at clay licks to spend hours watching colorful parrots eat dirt, which must be perplexing for the parrots.

lifer /'lī-fər/ ***noun:*** A species that a birder is seeing for the very first time. Outside of birding, this term has at least two other common definitions: someone serving a life sentence within the carceral system or someone who has spent their life as part of the armed forces. If you hear someone shout "That's a lifer!" use context clues to figure out which of the three definitions applies. If the person is pointing at a bird, it's probably the first one.

lifer pie /ˈlī-fər ˈpī/ *noun:* A slice of pie eaten in celebration of finding a **LIFER**. (This term was coined by Kimberly Kaufman, expert birder and co-founder of an Ohio-based event called the Biggest Week in American Birding.) When Biggest Week festival attendees find a bird species they haven't seen before, they visit a local restaurant called Blackberry Corners for a congratulatory pie slice. This tradition has spread far outside of Ohio, and all birders are encouraged to enjoy a dessert of any kind to celebrate a special sighting. If you're only just learning about this tradition, you may calculate all the uneaten slices of pie you've accrued and enjoy them now.

list /ˈlist/ *noun:* A record of all the species that a birder has seen in a particular area or during a certain timespan. Birders use apps or physical notebooks to keep yard lists, county lists, state lists, trip lists, year lists, life lists, and more. For a real challenge, keep every type of list so you can complete your list list.

lump /ˈləmp/ *verb:* To combine two or more species of birds into a single species based on new evidence. For instance, in 1973 the American Ornithological Society lumped the Red-shafted Flicker, Yellow-shafted Flicker, and Gilded Flicker into a single species, the Northern Flicker. Lumping can upset birders because they "lose" a bird they've sighted, reducing the number of species on their life list. It does, however, have its benefits. Consider this: If all birds were lumped into one species, we'd all have a completed list, and we'd finally be free to just chill or do whatever it is that other people do.

M

mega /ˈme-gə/ *noun:* A bird that has wandered far outside of its typical range and shows up in an area where it has never, or very rarely, been seen. For example, the Steller's Sea-Eagle is native to parts of Japan, North and South Korea, and eastern Russia, but in 2020, a single Steller's Sea-Eagle wandered into Alaska and flew across North America to New England and Atlantic Canada. Birders traveled from all over to see this incredible mega and add it to their life lists. Here are some helpful memory aids for remembering the word *mega*:

- **M**ajorly **E**xcitin**G** **A**vian
- **M**assive **E**agle **G**oing **A**WOL
- **M**e? I'm calling in sick because I'm going to go see the Stellar's Sea-**E**a**G**le, **A**ctually

memory /ˈmem-rē/ *noun:* Your mind's remarkable capacity to store a list of every bird species you've seen throughout your life coupled with its inability to retain your credit card number or the place where you just put your keys or phone.

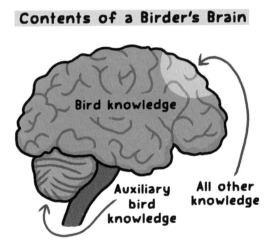

Contents of a Birder's Brain

Bird knowledge

Auxiliary bird knowledge

All other knowledge

Merlin /ˈmər-lən/ *noun:* **1.** A small falcon
native to much of the Northern Hemisphere.
2. A widely used app from the Cornell Lab
of Ornithology that, among other functions,
identifies birdsongs in real time. **3.** A mythical
wizard who, according to legend, helped
King Arthur identify birdsongs in real time,
propelling him to the top of the eBird rankings
and provoking so much jealousy that the
treacherous Mordred rose up against him in
a final, tragic war that destroyed Camelot.

metamorphosis /ˌme-tə-ˈmȯr-fə-səs/
noun: The biological process in which a rare
bird transforms itself into a common bird when
you lift up your binoculars to view it, point it
out to an expert, or look more closely at your
photos later.

migration /mī-ˈgrā-shən/ *noun:* A

phenomenon in which birds move back and forth across the landscape to take advantage of seasonal food abundances or good nesting sites. Some birds migrate short distances; the Greater Sage-Grouse, for example, travels up and down mountains to follow the seasonal growth of certain food plants. Other birds make long treks, such as the Arctic Tern, which flies from the Arctic to the Antarctic and back. Some bird species don't migrate at all. The Northern Cardinal is happy to stay in one place and cheer on other birds as they fly past on their migrations. If you listen carefully, you'll hear it quietly calling them a bunch of overachievers.

misidentify /ˌmis-ī-ˈden-tə-ˌfī/ *verb:* To
determine incorrectly that a bird belongs
to a particular species or is of a particular
sex or age. Every birder misidentifies birds
sometimes, and even expert birders make
mistakes. The author of this book has
personally witnessed experts misidentify a
Long-billed Dowitcher as a Wilson's Snipe,
a Western Sandpiper as a Semipalmated
Sandpiper, and a Great Blue Heron as a Bald
Eagle (to be fair, that bird was far away).
Once the author heard an expert exclaim,
"That's a Magnificent Frigatebird!" but as the
bird approached, it morphed into an Osprey
carrying an oddly shaped stick. You should
never feel bad for misidentifying a bird. If
anything, you should blame the birds for
stubbornly refusing to wear name tags.

mnemonic /ni-ˈmä-nik/ *noun:* A widely

used word, phrase, or collection of nonsense syllables that roughly corresponds to a bird's song and functions as a memory aid. For instance, birders remember the notes that make up an Eastern Towhee's refrain with the traditional mnemonic, "Drink your tea!" Some mnemonics are regionally specific. In the United States, the mnemonic for the White-throated Sparrow's song is *Old-Sam-Peabody-Peabody-Peabody*, but in Canada, it's *Oh-sweet-Canada-Canada-Canada*, and Canadian birders will defend that interpretation steadfastly, if politely. In an interesting shift, the White-throated Sparrow's song has changed in recent decades. Much of the population has switched to a shorter refrain and now sings *Old-Sam-Peabo-Peabo-Peabo* or *Oh-sweet Cana-Cana-Cana*, turning both phrases into nonsense. This shift has eased international tensions and both national governments have heralded it as a bold step toward peace.

mobbing /'mäb-iŋ/ *noun:* A behavior in which a smaller bird flies at a larger bird, often while calling, in an attempt to drive it out of the area. Many birds engage in mobbing behavior, including crows, blackbirds, kingbirds, jays, and chickadees. Birds of various species will gather together to mob a common enemy. If you find yourself being mobbed by birds, ask yourself: Am I too close to a nest? Should I back off? Should I stop stuffing all these tasty eggs into my mouth?

MODO /ˈmō-(ˌ)dō/ *noun:* A four-letter abbreviation of **MOURNING DOVE** drawn from the list of **ALPHA CODES**. You can use this abbreviation to alert other birders about a Mourning Dove without having to waste time on extra syllables. It'll work well until you inevitably encounter someone who does not know what an alpha code is, at which point you will have to expend far more syllables explaining bird codes and abbreviations and bird banding—so, on the whole, it is probably a wash. If you see a MODO that is half obscured by a branch or partially eaten by a Peregrine Falcon, it is a quasi-MODO.

molt /ˈmōlt/ ***verb:*** To shed and then regrow some or all feathers. Unable to purchase clothing at most stores, birds must instead molt regularly to keep looking fresh. ***noun:*** The period of time during which a bird sheds and regrows its feathers. The molt is a vulnerable, awkward, and energy-intensive period; some birds even lose the ability to fly during their molt. They cower on the ground, full of rage, glaring up at the firmament that is now denied them. Scientists, on the other hand, are sick weirdos who adore the molt, as patterns of plumage loss can indicate a bird's age and sex. They have developed a complex system of terminology to categorize the types of molts and determine the sequences in which feathers are replaced. They've even published entire books devoted to the science of the molt; apparently, some people have even read them. If birds knew about all of this, they'd be mortified.

moonwatching /ˈmün-ˌwä-chiŋ/ *noun:*

The act of gazing at the full moon to view birds during **MIGRATION**. Many birds travel under cover of darkness, including warblers, cuckoos, thrushes, and sparrows, but you can watch the moon and observe their silhouettes as they pass in front of its face. Be forewarned: If you stare at the full moon for too long during the migratory season, you may become a werewarbler, a hideous beast that is human by day but transforms into a songbird by night. You'll know you're a werewarbler if you go to sleep one night during a full moon and wake up the next morning in an insect-rich wildlife preserve thousands of miles away.

moorhen /ˈmu̇r-ˌhen/ *noun:* A roundish wading bird with absurdly long toes. The Eurasian Moorhen of Europe, Africa, and Asia was recently SPLIT from North America's Common Moorhen, which was renamed the Common Gallinule. Remember: If you're in the moors of Europe and you see a hen, that's a Common Moorhen. If you're in the galls of North America and you see a nule, that's a Common Gallinule.

morning /ˈmȯr-niŋ/ *noun:* The part of a birder's day that begins with a bleary pre-dawn drive to a local preserve. As the sun rises in the frigid air, they'll wade through wet grass and take grainy low-light pictures of tiny birds. Once the day becomes properly warm and dry and normal people start waking up, it's time to heave a happy sigh and, filled with a deep sense of satisfaction, head home and check for ticks.

morning flight /ˈmȯr-niŋ ˈflīt/ *noun:*

A phenomenon in which night-migrating birds continue to fly on for some time in the morning so that they can reach a good place to feed and rest. Some birders enjoy the challenge of identifying birds during the morning flight, when their quarry is soaring speedily overhead in the weak dawn light, making subtle flight calls instead of easily distinguishable songs. Identifying birds during morning flight is an inexact science; it's often a matter of blending various lines of evidence until an approximation is reached. But with some practice, anyone can learn to mix their knowledge of migratory habits with their fleeting observations of calls, colors, patterns, body shapes, sizes, and flying styles to succeed in giving themselves an enormous headache.

morph /ˈmȯrf/ *noun:* A term describing the two or more color forms that some species exhibit. Eastern Screech-Owls, for example, can have reddish or grayish plumage. Gouldian Finches can have black, red, or golden heads. Many hawks come in light and dark morphs, as well as intermediate variations. As with **HYBRIDS**, morphs evolved as a marketing tactic to keep people interested in birding once they've seen all the species. When you've observed every morph, you'll be eligible for a secret prize. (Spoiler: It's a **PELLET**.)

Eastern Screech-Owl

Red Morph

Party Morph

Gray Morph

Mourning Dove /ˈmȯr-niŋ ˌdəv/ *noun:*

A slender dove with a long, pointed tail that is found throughout much of North America, including in urban and suburban areas. Beginner birders often mistake its coos for the sounds of an owl; more experienced birders graduate to mistaking its shape for a falcon. Mourning Doves are notorious for nesting in terrible places, like porches out in the open, rain gutters, satellite dishes, or the tops of garage doors. Their nests often get raided by crows or simply blow away in a high wind. Scientists have not figured out how these birds successfully reproduce; they suspect that there's just a factory somewhere pumping them out.

movie /'mü-vē/ *noun:* A piece of media comprising moving pictures and sound, which is enjoyed by birders until they hear a bird call that doesn't match the scene's geographical area or habitat, at which point they're permanently distracted.

N

naturalist /ˈna-ch(ə-)rə-list/ *noun:*

Someone who is interested in every aspect of nature, from birds to insects to moss, and so is constantly distrac—*Whoa, look at that gorgeous wasp!*—ted by all of the many sights and sounds arou—*Ooh, do you smell that skunk?*—nd them. They are fun and informative to be around, even if they are also somewhat exhaus—*Wow, coyote poop!*—ting.

nemesis bird /'ne-mə-səs ˌbərd/ *noun:*

1. A bird species that you want to see but that keeps eluding you, despite the fact that you have put considerable effort into searching the proper habitat during the appropriate season and time of day. 2. A bird that you have angered to the point that you must one day meet it in a ritualistic combat from which only one of you will emerge alive. If you get a chance to choose your nemesis bird, pick a sparrow, a dove, or a Bushtit; do not select an eagle, a heron, or a Secretarybird.

nest /'nest/ *noun:* A structure in which a bird lays its eggs and cares for its young until they're old enough to head out into the world. Bird nests can vary from a Hooded Oriole's complex woven basket that hangs from the top of a tree, to a Piping Plover's scraped-out depression that sits in the sand and gravel on a beach, to a Rock Pigeon's two or three sticks tossed haphazardly on top of your air conditioner.

nictitating membrane /'nik-tə-ˌtā-tiŋ ˈmem-ˌbrān/ *noun:* An extra eyelid found in birds, as well as some fish, amphibians, reptiles, and mammals. This see-through membrane sweeps horizontally across the eye to protect or clean it without obscuring vision. Humans have nonfunctional, vestigial nictitating membranes. This provides incontrovertible proof that we're inferior to birds.

nocturnal flight call (NFC) recording /ˌen-(ˌ)ef-ˈsē ri-ˈkȯr-diŋ/ *verb:* To

digitally capture the sounds made by a bird that is migrating at night. Birders usually find it difficult to observe nocturnal migrations, on account of all the darkness. However, many species make brief, high-pitched NFCs to their flock members to maintain group cohesion. Birders have figured out how to set up specialized software and recording devices to capture these sounds. The next day, they carefully analyze the recordings to identify which species flew overhead. NFC recording gives birders a glimpse into a previously inaccessible world of wonders, allowing them to listen in as birds say things like *chirp* and *cheep* and *tseep* and *peep* and *I'mlost* and *Wowit'sreallydarkuphere.*

O

Oleaginous Hemispingus

/ō-lē-'a-jə-nəs ˌhe-mə-'spiŋ-gəs/ *noun:* The actual
English (not Latin) name of a bird species.
The Oleaginous Hemispingus is a dull
olive-yellow bird of the family Thraupidae
that lives in the mountains of northeastern
South America. Judging from its name, it is
presumably quite oily and has only half a
spingus, poor thing.

oology /ō-ˈä-lə-jē/ *noun:* The study of bird eggs. This term has Greek origins and may seem intimidating at first, but you'll memorize it easily once you notice that the written word contains three eggs—five, if you want to include umlauts. If a cowbird or cuckoo visits an existing nest and sneakily lays another egg in it, that's ooölogy.

ornithology /ˌȯr-nə-ˈthä-lə-jē/ *noun:*
The scientific study of birds. From the Latin
ornit, meaning "like a hornet," and *holog*y,
meaning "but with feathers."

owl /ˈau̇(-ə)l/ *noun:* A bird belonging to the
order Strigiformes. Its piercing, unbroken
gaze cuts into your soul and makes you feel
at once deeply connected to the world and
also unsettled by its profound mysteries,
though actually the owl is just using every
last one of its brain cells trying to figure out
if you're a mouse.

owling /ˈau̇(-ə)-liŋ/ *noun:* The practice of going outside when it's dark to look and listen for owls. Here are a few sounds to listen for while owling:

Sound	Sounds Like	Species
Cheerful whinny	A horse	Eastern Screech-owl
Soft, repetitive toot	A tiny choo-choo train	Northern Pygmy-Owl
Hideous screech	A harbinger of the apocalypse	Barn Owl
Hoot	An owl	Mourning Dove

oystercatcher /ˈȯi-stər-ˌka-chər/

noun: Any of twelve black and orange coastal bird species belonging to the family Haematopodidae. The name oystercatcher is quite misleading because 1) these birds eat a variety of mollusks, worms, and other small ocean creatures besides oysters, and 2) the suffix "catcher" makes some generous assumptions about the running speed of an oyster.

Get back here!

P

partial migration /ˈpär-shəl mī-ˈgrā-shən/

noun: A behavior in which only certain members of a species migrate to a different location outside of the breeding season, while others stay put. Some human New Englanders, for example, migrate to Florida for the winter, whereas others stay home to shovel out their driveways and pretend to enjoy cross-country skiing.

Patagonia Picnic Table Effect

/ˌpa-tə-ˈgō-nyə ˈpik-(ˌ)nik ˈtā-bəl i-ˈfekt/ *noun:* A phenomenon that occurs when someone spots a rare bird and birders flock to the area, leading to more sightings of rare species there. It is named after a picnic table at a rest stop south of Patagonia, Arizona. Researchers have failed to find empirical support for the effect. Nobody is in doubt, however, that the effect has led to greater awareness of Patagonia, Arizona.

patch /'pach/ *noun:* 1. A location near your home where you bird regularly throughout the year. Many birders maintain a "patch list" of species they've seen there. Focusing on a patch can help you learn more about your neighborhood, refine your knowledge of habitat, and deepen your understanding of local birds. 2. A small, beautifully embroidered insignia that birders purchase at a wildlife refuge or birding festival and attach to their clothing as a souvenir of the experience. Many preserves and festivals sell patches as a means of fundraising. 3. A nondescript piece of fabric that you sew onto your clothes after you lose a pitched battle with some greenbriar or multiflora rose.

peep /ˈpēp/ *noun:* A small, brownish shorebird that makes a peeping sound and belongs to one of several similar-looking species. Birders differ in their opinions as to which species count as peeps. Some feel that the list should include Least, Semipalmated, and Western Sandpipers, plus Little, Temminck's, Red-necked, and Long-toed Stints. Others add in the longer-winged White-rumped and Baird's Sandpipers. Some include Dunlins and Sanderlings. Further complicating matters, a few birders expand the definition to fold in any small shorebird that's hard to identify. If you want to be especially chaotic, use this term for any bird that peeps, including the Osprey or Bald Eagle. In fact, if you yourself can produce a peeping sound, go ahead and add your name to the list. You may lose some birding friends, but you'll gain Osprey friends if you peep loud enough.

pelagic /pə-ˈla-jik/ *noun:* A trip that is very much like a cruise, except that the boat is less comfortable, there's no pool, you'll probably get seasick, you'll sleep in a bunk, and you'll get simultaneously sunburned, wind-burned, and frozen, so it's actually not like a cruise at all. You will, however, observe many rare and beautiful seabirds, plus sunfish, whales, flying fish, Portuguese man o' wars, and other wildlife that the open sea can offer. You'll return with an empty stomach but a full life list. The typical call of a birder on a pelagic sounds like "What a great—*bleaughhhhhh*—pelagic. I'm having such an amazing—*heuuuurghh*—time."

pellet /'pe-lət/ *noun:* A blob of indigestible critter parts, including bones, fur, or shell, that is barfed up by a bird after it eats. Gulls, eagles, hawks, owls, and other birds puke up pellets. When birders come across pellets lying on the ground, they are compelled to stop and pick them apart, exclaiming "Ooh, I found a tooth!" or "Wow, a whole mouse skull!" with the glee of Dr. Frankenstein shopping for parts.

P

pish /'pish/ *verb:* The act of making a *pshhh pshhh* sound with your mouth to mimic the alarm calls of songbirds. When you pish, one of two things will happen: Either a spectacular flock of songbirds will surround you, filling your heart with joy, or absolutely nothing will happen and your pishes will sputter out until you stand in silent humiliation. Good luck!

plastic owl /'pla-stik 'aủ(-ə)l/ *noun:* A life-sized fake owl installed on a building to keep pests away. Fake owls are highly effective, provided that your goals are 1) to decorate your building with a plastic owl, 2) to confuse and disappoint nearby birders, and 3) to give pigeons a pleasantly rounded perch upon which to poop.

playback /ˈplā-ˌbak/ *noun:* A prerecorded tape or digital file of bird sounds—such as screech owl trills or chickadee alarm calls—used to coax wild birds into the open so that birders can view them. The use of playback is nuanced, ethically complex, and, in some places, illegal. A full and fair discussion of the associated issues is beyond the scope of this book. As a general rule, though, it's considered unethical to hide behind a tree and use playback to lure in your birder friends so you can chuckle at them when they can't find the screech owl.

pop up /ˈpäp-ˌəp/ *verb:* To suddenly appear and then disappear. This is a behavior performed by birds that are foraging deep within some foliage; they will hop out into the open for the precise amount of time that it takes you to say "It just popped up!" and begin to hoist your camera or binoculars.

precocial /pri-ˈkō-shəl/ *adjective:* Hatching out with open eyes and a full coat of down feathers. A precocial chick grows up very fast, so it can scurry out of the nest shortly after hatching, sending the parents dashing after it across the beach or forest floor to give it some pointers before it tries to drive a car or sign up for a credit card.

How to Photograph a Bird That Pops Up

preen gland /ˈprēn gland/ *noun:* A gland located above a bird's tail that secretes an oily substance; also known as the uropygial gland. When a bird preens, it uses its beak to rub this oily secretion on its feathers, helping to smooth its plumage and adding an element of waterproofing. The oil is also important for avian communication; for instance, Crested and Whiskered Auklets produce a characteristic tangerine scent that may originate from the preen gland. Humans can smell a flock of these auklets from a kilometer or more downwind. Whenever you smell citrus, be sure to glance around you; either someone is peeling an orange or you're about to fall prey to a flock of auklets.

primary projection /ˈprī-ˌmer-ē

prə-ˈjek-shən/ *noun:* 1. The distance that a bird's primary feathers stretch beyond the secondary or tertial feathers when the wing is folded; a useful identification tip. 2. The projected results of a primary election. Don't get these two terms confused or you might wind up with a White-rumped Sandpiper as president.

P

pronunciation /prə-ˌnən(t)-sē-ˈā-shən/

noun: A contentious subject amongst birders. A handful of bird-related terms have multiple commonly used pronunciations; for instance, some birders say "plover" so that it rhymes with "over," and others say it so that it rhymes with "lover." Additional controversial words include *murre*, *gyrfalcon*, *parula*, *niche*, and *pileated*. Here's a helpful guide to pronouncing these words correctly:

Word	Say it like...
Plover	Plover
Murre	Murre
Gyrfalcon	Gyrfalcon
Parula	Parula
Niche	Niche
Pileated	Pileated

ptarmigan /ˈtär-mi-gən/ *noun:* One of three pterribly named species of the genus *Lagopus* that are native to the ptundra. The word *ptarmigan* did not initially start with a *p*. It came from the Scottish Gaelic name for the Willow Ptarmigan, *tarmachan*. In the 1600s, English writers added the *p* because they thought that the word sounded Greek, as in the Greek word *pterón*, meaning "wing." This ptroubling ptypo has forever ptarnished the ptarmigan's repuptaption and left everyone ptermanently ptongue-ptied.

pun /ˈpən/ *noun:* A joke whose humor relies on using a word that has multiple meanings or on a word that sounds like another word. Birders both love and hate puns—they can be funny but also groan-worthy. Wren considering whether to deploy a pun or knot, take stork of the situation and consider owl the consequences. Is your contribution guan to contribute to the con-veery-sation? Willet tern out okay, such that everyone will think you're funny from heron out, or will people think you're oriole piece of work? What trogon to do if the experience leaves you bittern and full of egrets? You'll likely decide that there are better ways to spindalis time.

Pyrrhuloxia /ˌpir-(y)ə-ˌläk-sē-ə/ *noun:*

A cardinal native to northern Mexico and parts of the US southwest that, much like the **PTARMIGAN**, has an exceedingly awkward name. The French naturalist Charles Lucien Bonaparte appears to have coined the word *Pyrrhuloxia* because he thought that this bird was most closely related to the bullfinch genus *Pyrrhula* and the crossbill genus *Loxia*. It was not. Sadly, this hideous portmanteau has stood the test of time, vexing anyone who tries to pronounce it. There are, in fact, two correct pronunciations: "Pyrr[indistinct mumbling]" and "THAT one THERR."

R

rail /ˈrāl/ *noun:* A mysterious swamp monster that hides deep in the reeds and occasionally screams. Scientists tell us that rails are long-legged, ground-dwelling birds with rounded wings, but they're lying because nobody has ever seen one.

range /ˈrānj/ *noun:* The geographic area where you can find a particular bird species, provided that the time of year is suitable, habitat destruction hasn't pushed it out, climate change hasn't driven it into new areas, and it hasn't decided to hide because it personally dislikes you.

raptor /ˈrap-tər/ *noun:* A bird of prey with a hooked beak and sharp talons such as a hawk, an eagle, or a falcon. This term should not be confused with 1) a nickname for the dinosaur velociraptor, popularized by the *Jurassic Park* franchise, or 2) a member of Toronto's NBA team. Unlike movie dinosaurs, most hawks cannot open doors, and their free throw percentages are nothing to write home about, either.

RB Nut /ˌär-ˈbē ˈnət/ *noun:* A nickname for the Red-breasted Nuthatch, a small songbird that creeps up and down tree bark. If the Red-breasted Nuthatch is your favorite bird, you're an RB Nut nut. If you're a fan of the Red-breasted Nuthatch and also fast food, you're an Arby's RB Nut nut. If you're a fan of the Red-breasted Nuthatch and also fast food and you run a small inn that's temporarily closed but will reopen soon, you're an Arby's B&B (brb) RB Nut nut.

record shot /ˈre-kərd ˈshät/ *noun:* A

bad photo of a good bird; also known as a "doc shot." Sometimes you catch a quick glimpse of a rare species, and you're only able to snap one or two blurry, distant, or poorly lit shots as proof of your sighting. When you post the images online, be sure to label them "record shots" to reassure people that they don't reflect your typical photography skills—you're just sharing them to provide a record of your observation. If you're a really bad photographer, label all your photos "record shots" and see if anyone notices.

rehabber /ˈrē-ˌha-bər/ *noun:* Someone who cares for injured and sick birds out of the goodness of their heart, the power of their convictions, and the strength of their tolerance for bird secretions; short for wildlife rehabilitator. Rehabbers heal birds from all sorts of injuries. They care for those that have flown into windows, suffered an attack from an outdoor cat, or are sick from gunshot wounds, lead, or rat poison. They raise chicks whose parents have died, and if all goes well, they release their charges into the wild. They do all of this even though the task is thankless and heartbreaking. Not all heroes wear capes; some wear vulture puke.

reviewer /ri-ˈvyü-ər/ *noun:* A volunteer who evaluates observations that are submitted to the Cornell Lab of Ornithology's eBird database. When people report sightings of birds that are especially rare for the area or the season, eBird automatically flags them and a reviewer takes a closer look to make sure the reports are correct. For example, say a wildly inaccurate birder reports 4 trillion Emperor Penguins in Lake Erie in July. In this case, the sighting would be flagged and a reviewer would reject it, because 4 trillion Emperor Penguins—each weighing an average of 88 pounds—would raise Lake Erie by 20 feet, flooding the nearby city of Toledo, Ohio (with a population of approximately 269,000), and a simple call to the mayor of Toledo would reveal that the city is still above water.

ringtone /ˈriŋ-ˌtōn/ *noun:* A sound that a phone makes to signal that someone is calling. Birders tend to use their favorite birdsongs as ringtones, which works just fine when they're birding alone but can cause all sorts of hilarious chaos at birding gatherings. If you hear a bird song, trace the source of the sound and be aware that the only bird that even vaguely resembles a cell phone in shape is the Greater Lophorina (*Lophorina superba*).

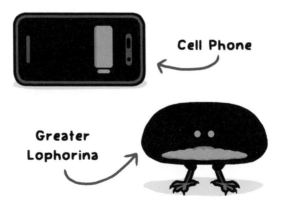

Cell Phone

Greater
Lophorina

S

scan /'skan/ *verb:* To park yourself in one place, stare through binoculars or a scope, and move your field of view very slowly across the landscape, methodically checking each lump of sand to see if it's a sandpiper or each gull to determine whether it's a rare one. If you get bored, which you inevitably will, imagine that you're an elite robot who was sent from the future to scan your surroundings and terminate any threats. Try making little *beep-boop* sounds, if it helps.

scope /'skōp/ *noun:* Short for spotting scope, a contraption that's like a telescope but is used for looking at birds. A scope is expensive, finicky, and heavy, and you can't use it while you're walking around. It does, however, have much better magnification than binoculars. No other device will give you such exquisite views of that plastic bag you thought was a Snowy Owl.

seabird /'sē-ˌbərd/ *noun:* A bird that gazed upon the sea with its violent storms, endless roiling waves, lack of shelter, and extreme temperatures—plus sharks, colossal squids, deadly jellyfish, and other assorted horrors of the deep—and said, "This seems like a nice place to live."

A Seabird At Home

seawatching /'sē-ˌwä-chiŋ/ *noun:* The act of standing by the ocean and staring at the waves for hours on end, squinting through the fog and spray while the wind burns your face and the salt blurs your glasses, so that you can briefly glimpse an interesting seabird zooming past. Seawatching is like waiting in a line in the rain for hours and hours so you can get your favorite musician's autograph, but with more murres.

"seen anything good?" /sēn ˈe-nē-thiŋ ˈgu̇d/ *noun:* The customary call by which birders greet each other. When identifying a birder, be aware that there are several variant calls. Here are some greetings you may hear:

Call	Caller
"Any warblers today?"	Birder
"Wow, that camera is gigantic! Are you some kind of spy?"	Nonbirder
"What are you on?"	Birder or someone who wants to purchase illegal substances
"Teacher, teacher, teacher, teacher!"	Ovenbird or overly enthusiastic ornithology student
"Who cooks for you?"	Birder or Barred Owl or person who wants to send their compliments to the chef
"I like birds, but I'm not really a *birder.* I have trouble telling empids apart, and I don't know my flight calls."	Birder

shorb /ˈshȯrb/ *noun:* A nickname for a shorebird. Like a **BORB**, but wetter.

shorebird /ˈshȯr-ˌbərd/ *noun:* A bird that 1) spends time near the shore and 2) belongs to the scientific order Charadriiformes but 3) isn't a **GULL**, a **TERN**, or an **ALCID**, even though those birds belong to Charadriiformes and often hang out by the shore. Note: Some shorebirds do not spend time at the actual shore; the Upland Sandpiper, for example, prefers uplands. If you think that this whole thing is confusing, you're right—it shore is.

S

skulky /ˈskəl-kē/ *adjective:* Shy, retiring, and difficult to see; referring to a bird that sneaks around in the brush, offering a birder just the briefest of looks. Many birds can be skulky, including rails, wrens, thrushes, and certain warblers and sparrows. If you try to photograph a skulky bird, the resulting images will probably fail to impress other birders. The photos will, however, delight any nearby botanists, who will enjoy identifying all the green stuff that's in the way.

skunked /ˈskəŋkt/ *adjective:* 1. Having failed to see a bird. 2. Having been sprayed by a skunk. Both conditions are unpleasant, but the second one is preferable because you at least got to observe a mammal.

snood /'snüd/ *noun:* The naked, erectile lump of flesh on a turkey's forehead. It can stick up like a hideously gnarled unicorn horn or droop down like a meaty teardrop, and it changes color from salami-red to corpse-blue depending on a turkey's arousal and anxiety levels. Female turkeys prefer males with longer snoods. This word and its definition are best invoked when you're in a dull conversation and you'd like to bring it to an abrupt end.

A Guide to Turkey Lumps

- Snood
- Wattle
- Caruncles

songbird /'sȯŋ-ˌbərd/ *noun:* Colloquially, any bird that sings a pretty song; scientifically, any member of the bird suborder Passeri. Birds belonging to that suborder have a complex set of muscles that give them exquisite control of their syrinx, a sound-producing organ, and are able to learn and perfect songs over time. Note: Crows are technically in Passeri, but their songs are enjoyable only if you're a goth or a fan of the all-crow experimental noise rock band Corrupted Cloacas.

sp. /'spə/ *noun:* A short form of the word *species*. Say it *spuh* like you're trying to eject an errant gnat from your mouth. When you can't identify a bird species, just use sp. For example, if you're looking at a flock of confusing warblers, say warbler sp. If you're just very tired today, go with bird sp. Let's be honest—there are a lot of birds.

spark bird /ˈspärk ˌbərd/ *noun:* **1.** The bird that first sparks a love of birding in an individual, sending them on the path toward a lifelong hobby of observing and appreciating the avian world. **2.** Any bird that routinely and enthusiastically commits arson.

sparrow /ˈsper-(ˌ)ō/ *noun:* One of a number of small, brownish or grayish birds that you may initially dismiss when you start birding. Over time, you'll start to notice that sparrows have different body shapes, particular songs, and subtly unique coloration. They'll creep inexorably into your psyche until one day you'll pick out a Clay-colored Sparrow amidst the Chipping Sparrows (which are slightly grayer) and you'll feel like you're strong enough to punch the sun.

species richness /ˈspē-(ˌ)shēz

ˈrich-nəs/ **noun: 1.** A tally of the species living in a particular area; more species equals greater species richness. **2.** The total wealth possessed by a species. If you're birding and you see an expensive black town car pull up, and out steps a glamorous but aloof warbler carrying a Louis Vuitton bag full of spiders, that warbler has high species richness.

spectrogram /ˈspek-t(r)ə-ˌgram/ *noun:*
A visual representation of a bird's call or
song that shows the signal strength and
frequency over time. Studying spectrograms
is an excellent activity for those who want
to become better birders, love graphs and
spreadsheets, or enjoy staring at impenetrable
works of abstract expressionism.

speculum /ˈspe-kyə-ləm/ *noun:* 1. A colorful,
often iridescent patch on the secondary
feathers of a duck's wing. 2. A tool that a doctor
uses to examine various orifices. Don't be
confused! If you hear a birder say "Wow, look
at that gorgeous speculum," they're probably
talking about a duck and not a gynecologist.
(Plus, most duck doctors are quacks.)

split /'split/ *verb:* To divide a single bird species into two or more species based on new evidence, such as genetic analysis. For instance, in 2021 the American Ornithological Society split the Mew Gull into the Short-billed Gull and Common Gull. Splitting can disorient birders because it makes old field guides obsolete and messes with life lists. Even more upsetting is the fact that the entire concept of "species" is complex and messy. Considering that so many birds routinely hybridize, that evolution works on all sorts of scales, and that microorganisms regularly exchange genetic material without regard for labels, what then counts as a species? Why do humans feel compelled to create categories when the universe is just a sea of particles that occasionally coagulate into short-lived clumps of sentience, then dissipate back into the whole? Are we all just monkeys imposing our fragile narratives onto a chaotic and uncaring universe? What's the point of everything? I should really give my folks a call.

staging area /ˈstā-jiŋ ˈer-ē-ə/ *noun:*

1. A location at which migratory birds gather to rest and eat in preparation for **MIGRATION**.

2. A location at which migratory birds gather to put on a small play. Some of their favorite theatrical productions include *Who's Afraid of Virginia's Warbler*, *Waiting for Godwit*, and *The Taming of the Smew*.

stakeout /ˈstāk-ˌau̇t/ *noun:* A gathering of birders at the last known location of a rare bird. The word evokes detective-movie vibes, but a bird stakeout mostly involves waiting in a damp field, shifting from foot to foot, looking at the sky or the trees until your eyes ache, and occasionally making awkward conversation. When the suspect finally appears, the action really picks up: Everybody looks through their binoculars and whispers "wow."

stopover /ˈstäp-ˌō-vər/ *noun:* 1. A location or site where a bird can pause during a migration to eat and rest in safety. Birds rely on habitats such as marshes, shores, and forests to maintain the necessary levels of energy and alertness for their journey. 2. A location where a birder can pause during a trip to eat and rest in safety. Birders rely on habitats such as cafés, diners, and pastry shops to maintain the necessary levels of enthusiasm, caffeination, and a light dusting of powdered sugar for their journey.

strap /'strap/ *noun:* A strip of fabric or leather that attaches to your binoculars, backpack, or camera. The laws of physics state that, over time, any one strap will interlace with all adjacent straps until you're trapped in a web of cloth, like the prey of an enormous spider.

stringer /'striŋ-ər/ *noun:* Someone who sends other birders on a wild goose chase, sometimes literally. A stringer consistently reports false bird sightings. Many stringers aren't malicious; they're just overconfident. For instance, a stringer may see a large accipiter in a brief flyover and declare that it's a goshawk, dismissing the more likely possibility that it's a Cooper's Hawk. Unfortunately, some stringers intentionally falsify sightings of rare birds, sending local birders through dense brush or deep snow to find a bird that doesn't exist. If you do this, please stop. The other birders will figure you out, and, reputationally, your goose will be cooked.

sun /ˈsən/ *noun:* A massive star that, on the one hand, warms us, powers photosynthesis, and gives life to all the creatures on Earth, but, on the other hand, is a bright object that birds love to fly directly in front of when you're following them with your binoculars.

sunning /ˈsə-niŋ/ *noun:* A behavior in which birds bask in the sun. Sunning birds can assume alarming positions, such as spreading out flat on the ground, stretching out one wing, and half rolling over. They look injured or dead, which can cause worried birders to approach and startle them. Birds can avoid this embarrassing experience by wearing cool sunglasses to make it clear they're just chilling.

supercilium /ˌsüpə(r)ˈsilēəm/ *noun:* The set of feathers on the sides of a bird's head that arc above and behind its eyes. These feathers are often colorful, making them a distinctive and useful field mark. Many birders prefer the term "eyebrow," since using the word *supercilium* in regular conversation can make one sound supercilious.

T

target species /ˈtär-gət ˈspē-(ˌ)shēz/

noun: 1. A species that you aim to see during a particular outing. 2. A bird that wanders into a Target store. To help this bird find an exit, you can open a single large door, window, or other egress, close the other potential exit points, and shut off the lights. Then, leave the animal undisturbed until it escapes or finds its way to the checkout and successfully purchases its throw pillows and other affordably priced home essentials.

Spotted Sandpiper

teeter

teeter

teeter

teeter-peep /ˈtē-tər-ˈpēp/ *noun:* A
nickname for the Spotted Sandpiper, a
shorebird that makes a teetering motion as it
walks. The Spotted Sandpiper is also called
the teeter-bird, teeter-snipe, perk-bird, and
jerk-bird, and you should only use that last
nickname if you have a personal vendetta
against an individual Spotted Sandpiper.

tern /ˈtərn/ *noun:* Like a GULL, but pointier.

thrush /ˈthrəsh/ *noun:* One of a variety of birds in the family Turdidae, many of which make astonishingly complex songs. Some thrushes have bold markings, like the Varied Thrush, and others are subtly patterned, like the Hermit Thrush. Many are quite shy and **SKULKY**, preferring to hide in the underbrush. If you've never heard of a thrush and you'd like to find an image of one on the internet, exercise caution when doing a search; this term also refers to a human fungal infection. You should also be careful when searching for images of birds such as screamers, coots, coquettes, creepers, and boobies.

tick /'tik/ *noun:* 1. A new entry in a personal **LIST** of bird species seen. 2. A parasitic mite that crawls up your leg while you're busy finding birds. Take a close look at your new blood-sucking friend to see if it belongs to a species you haven't yet encountered. You might earn yourself a tick tick.

trash bird /'trash ˌbərd/ *noun:* An unfortunate term for a bird that is abundant to the point of being boring, at least to some birders. A trash bird may clog up your eBird list and crowd out other species at feeders. Examples of so-called trash birds include the House Sparrow, Rock Dove, and American Robin. Sometimes rare birds show up at actual trash dumps, and birders rush there in droves, searching for that wayward Common Shelduck, Slaty-backed Gull, or Smooth-billed Ani. These aren't considered trash birds; they just happen to be knee-deep in trash for perfectly respectable reasons.

tree /ˈtrē/ *noun:* A large plant that produces the oxygen we need to breathe and provides abundant perches and foraging locations for birds, but also grows twigs and leaves that obstruct our views of said birds, so it's sort of a mixed bag, much like the SUN.

trill /ˈtril/ *noun:* A birdsong consisting of quick syllables that blend together into an almost mechanical whirr. Birds that make trills include the Dark-eyed Junco, Pine Warbler, and Chipping Sparrow, and their songs can sound quite similar. With some practice, you might convince yourself that you can tell these trills apart. You can use qualitative words like *tinny* or *musical* or *swelling* to describe them with confidence. You can find yourself going about life with an air of superiority, buoyed by the strength of your convictions, greeting your fellow birders with a winning smile, until one day an unusual-sounding Chipping Sparrow throws you into a tailspin.

tubenose /ˈtüb-ˌnōz/ *noun:* Birds in the order Procellariiformes that have tube-like sheaths enclosing their nostrils, including albatrosses, petrels, storm-petrels, and shearwaters. One of the best things about birding is that you get to say "tubenose" with a straight face.

tube

TV /'tē-'vē/ *noun:* Short for Turkey Vulture, a large, soaring, carrion-eating bird of North America. If you're watching a Turkey Vulture fly through the sky, and you find that you can't tear your eyes away because the whole scene is a deeply entertaining yet thought-provoking reflection of modern society, that's called prestige TV.

Tyrant Flycatcher /'tī-rənt 'flī-ˌka-chər/ *noun:* A bird in the family Tyrannidae. Some Tyrant Flycatchers can be especially aggressive, which is why they're labeled "tyrants." To be fair, few bird families have spent the time to hash out a binding constitution that would curb a leader's absolute power.

U

upending /ˌəp-ˈen-diŋ/ *noun:* A feeding behavior in which a duck points its head down so that its butt sticks straight up in the air; also known as mooning.

usual suspects, the /ˈyü-zhə-wəl ˈsə-ˌspekts thə/ *noun:* 1. The typical species one expects to find at a particular location. 2. A 1995 mystery film that will beguile you with its tight plotting and twist ending but will disappoint you with its relative lack of birds.

V

vireo /ˈvir-ē-ˌō/ *noun:* A small songbird of the family Vireonidae. Vireos and **WOOD-WARBLERS** look alike. To tell them apart, observe their bills: Warblers have slender, tapering bills, whereas vireos have thicker, blunter bills with a slightly hooked tip. Warblers have small feet and a slender body shape, whereas vireos have larger feet and a thicker chest. Warbler songs are short, concise, and self-contained, whereas vireo songs go on and on.*

---

* And on and on [*pause for a quick preen*] and on and on and on and on and on and on and on and on and on and on and on and on and on and on and on and on.

vocal mimicry /ˈvō-kəl ˈmi-mi-krē/

noun: **1.** A behavior in which a bird copies the calls and songs of other birds. For instance, Blue Jays mimic the screams of various hawk species. **2.** A behavior in which new birders copy the slang of more seasoned birders until they find that they cannot stop saying weird things like "Look at the primary projections on those peeps. And what lovely tubenoses—I haven't seen that many since my last pelagic."

vocal repertoire /ˈvō-kəl ˈre-pər-ˌtwär/
noun: The entire collection of sounds produced
by a bird, including its songs, calls, burps,
farts, and, in the case of a middle-aged bird,
the grunting sound that it makes when it gets
up after a long sit.

vulture /ˈvəl-chər/ *noun:* A bird of prey
that, out of politeness, waits for its prey to
die of natural causes before eating it.

W

warbler neck /ˈwȯr-blər ˌnek/ *noun:*

A painful muscular condition caused by spending hours looking up into the tops of trees for warblers. Warbler neck afflicts millions of birders per year and is comorbid with conditions such as vulture-roost stink-nose, telephoto-lens lower back, and binocular-strap chafe.

whale watch /ˈ(h)wāl ˈwäch/ *noun:*

A boat trip that provides excellent seabird viewing opportunities, provided the whales don't jump out of the water and block your view of the birds.

whitewash /ˈ(h)wīt-ˌwȯsh/ *noun:* Streaks

of white bird poop that encrust rocks or trees.
Like humans, birds produce toxic ammonia
as a waste product, but humans convert that
ammonia into urea, dilute it with water, and
pee it out, whereas birds convert it into uric
acid, which is lighter—helpful for flying—
and requires less water. The resulting waste
is a whitish goo or paste. Birders look for
whitewash to find hidden nests and determine
where birds regularly perch. *verb:* An attempt
to hide the grim truth with a thin veneer of
respectability, like calling bird poop stains
"whitewash."

window /ˈwin-(ˌ)dō/ *noun:* A sheet of
transparent solid material that, as far as
birds know, doesn't exist until they fly into
it. Frankly, it's rude of humans to make
certain bits of air unexpectedly hard. You
can help prevent window-related injuries or
deaths by applying specially made film or
tape to the outside of your windows, installing
outdoor screens, or hanging strings in front of
windows. Any bare parts of window should
be no more than 2 inches (5 cm) wide, so that
smaller birds won't try to fly between the
strings or pieces of tape. These solutions are
a win-win; birds survive, and humans get
GOOD LOOKS at them through those ridiculous
sheets of impenetrable air.

wing /'wiŋ/ *noun:* A modified forearm that, in the case of most birds, facilitates flight. To determine whether you have wings, try this simple test: Flap your forearms as hard as you can. If you rise up into the air, you've got wings and you may be a bird (or a bat). If you stay on the ground, you don't have wings unless you're an ostrich, a rhea, an emu, a penguin, a kiwi, a Kakapo, a cassowary, or one of the flightless rails, grebes, steamers, or cormorants.

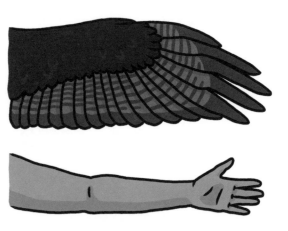

wood-warbler /ˈwu̇d ˌwȯr-blər/ *noun:*

A bird belonging to the family Parulidae; often shortened to warbler, but officially called wood-warbler to distinguish it from the distantly related European warblers. Wood-warblers are similar to the collectible creatures in the popular video game franchise Pokémon. They come in many colors and patterns, they're found in a wide variety of habitats, and they sing unique songs. Once you've seen one, you'll be compelled to find them all. Be aware, however, that to capture wood-warblers and train them to do battle in an arena is a violation of the Migratory Bird Treaty Act of 1918.

woodcock /ˈwu̇d-ˌkäk/ *noun:* A shorebird belonging to the genus *Scolopax* that has an unfortunate English name. It also goes by:

- Timberdoodle
- Night Partridge
- Big-eye
- Bogsucker
- Mudbat

If woodcocks ever learn English, they will destroy us.

woodpecker /ˈwu̇d-ˌpe-kər/ ***noun:*** One of a group of birds of the family Picidae that have a variety of characteristics and plumages, but, most importantly, can chop a hole in a tree using only their face.

wren /ˈren/ ***noun:*** One of several species in the family Troglodytidae that sing songs with power that is far out of proportion with their body size. Approximately 90 percent of a wren's internal anatomy consists of a large speaker and a megaphone, and 10 percent comprises the rest of its internal organs, plus storage space for tasty bugs.

X

X /'eks/ *noun:* What you can use when you're recording your bird sightings with the eBird app and you're having a difficult time determining the number of individuals of a species that you've seen. If that number is large and you don't have time to count all the birds, you can input X instead. The Cornell Lab of Ornithology discourages the use of X and urges birders to at least make a rough estimate. Therefore, you should only use X if a broad guess is impossible, or if you just want to indicate that you gave a particular bird a little kiss.

Y

yodel /ˈyō-dᵊl/ *noun:* 1. A unique form of human singing that involves switching rapidly and regularly between low and high pitches. 2. The territorial call of a male loon. The fact that both humans and loons yodel is an excellent example of **CONVERGENT EVOLUTION**.

yump /ˈyəmp/ *noun:* A nickname for the Yellow-rumped Warbler that sounds like a gastrointestinal malfunction, but still seems less objectionable than **BUTTERBUTT**.

Z

zugunruhe /ˈ(t)sù-kən-ˌrü-ə/ *noun:* 1. A term borrowed from a German word describing the seasonal, anxious motions of birds that are getting ready for **MIGRATION**; also known as migratory restlessness. They may hop about, jump from perch to perch, or flutter. 2. The seasonal, anxious motions of birders who are getting ready for migration. They may hop about, jump from perch to perch, or blow a paycheck on a scope.

zygodactyl /ˌzī-gə-ˈdak-təl/ *adjective:*
Describes a quality of a bird's foot having
four toes, with two toes (the second and third)
pointing forward and the other two pointing
backward. Birds with zygodactyl feet include
woodpeckers, cuckoos, owls, toucans, the
Osprey, most parrots, and others. You should
do your best to find and observe these birds
so that you have an excuse to say "zygodactyl"
as often as possible.

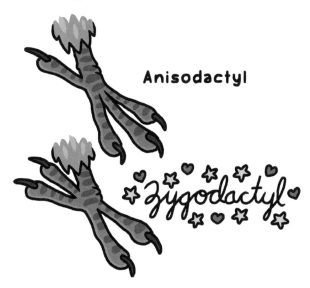

Anisodactyl

Zygodactyl